STORY TELLER

WRITTEN BY

COLIN BOYNTON

ISBN: 978-0-9559931-5-2

COPYRIGHT : COLIN BOYNTON 2017

INDEX

1. WHERE'S THE LIGHT?
2. WHEN IT'S SPRING AGAIN.
3. FORGOTTEN
4. GAMES WE PLAY
5. ?
6. JOURNEY
7. FOUND TREASURES
8. BERTIE
9. IS IT JUST ME?
10. MODERN MAN
11. THINKING
12. ESCAPE PLAN
13. MANKIND
14. LOYALTY
15. WHERE ARE THEY NOW?
16. WHO, WHEN, WHY?
17. BUT
18. SPRINGTIME
19. THE WRONG QUEUE
20. THERE IS...
21. WHO DECIDES?
22. GROWING OLDER
23. TRILOGY
24. BEWARE
25. IT MUST HAVE BEEN PT 1

26. IT MUST HAVE BEEN PT 2
27. IT MUST HAVE BEEN PT 3
28. IT MUST HAVE BEEN PT 4
29. IT MUST HAVE BEEN PT 5
30. IT MUST HAVE BEEN PT 6
31. IT MUST HAVE BEEN PT 7
32. SIMPLE THINGS
33. DEAF, DUMB & BLIND
34. EVERY DAY...ANOTHER DAY
35. TO THE MEMORY OF THE FALLEN...
36. MEMORY BOX
37. YOUNG AT HEART
38. NIGHT RIDER
39. TO LIVE AND BE FREE
40. I BELIEVE...
41. ALL INNOCENCE
42. FRED 2
43. SOMETHING FOR NOTHING – IT'S FREE!
44. DO YOU KNOW WHERE YOU'RE GOING TO?
45. YOUR MAJESTY.
46. ANOTHER DAY.
47. A WISH...
48. A WINTER LOVE STORY
49. TONIGHT, TONIGHT AND EVERYNIGHT
50. CHANGES

51. WHAT WE DID...
52. AS YEARS GO BY.
53. FAMILY TREE
54. MY TOWN
55. LONG MAY IT CONTINUE
56. GOING, GOING ALMOST GONE...
57. FORGET ME NOTS
58. THE CREEPER
59. A CRY : A PLEA
60. THE APPROACH
61. HOME
62. ANOTHER SIDE
63. AUTOBIOGRAPHY
64. LONG FORGOTTEN HERO
65. AUTUMN LEAVES A MEMORY
66. DO YOU REMEMBER...?
67. TRAVELS IN MY LIFE.
68. HEARTBREAK EXPRESS.
69. DON'T ASK...I DIDN'T.
70. TRUST
71. WHEN AN ANGEL CALLS
72. SSSSSSHHH!
73. TRAVELLER
74. IF...
75. T – T – F – N !

1. WHERE'S THE LIGHT?

IT'S DARK AND DULL
IT'S MISERABLE,
IT'S WINTER ONCE AGAIN.
I'D LIKE SOME FUN
OUT IN THE SUN,
NOT IN THE POURING RAIN.
IT'S COLD AND WET
THE WIND BLOWS YET,
WILL THERE SOON BE SNOW?
THE BOGGY GROUND
MAKES THE
SOUND,
OF WATERLOGGED BELOW.
IT'S DARK AND GREY
THROUGHOUT THE DAY,
AND SOON IT WILL BE NIGHT.
AS DARKNESS FALLS
OUTSIDE THESE WALLS,
I STILL KEEP ON THE LIGHT

ALL DAY!

2. WHEN IT'S SPRING AGAIN.

I HEAR A BLACKBIRD SINGING
AT THE BREAK OF DAY,
SITTING ON THE GARDEN FENCE
HE'S WHISTLING AWAY.
I SEE THE EARLY RAY OF SUN
PEEP ABOVE THE TREES
BEHIND THE GENTLE SWAYING BRANCHES
IN THE MORNING BREEZE.
I SEE A YELLOW DAFFODIL
THAT'S JUST BEGUN TO FLOWER
IT'S TRUMPET PEEPING THROUGH THE PETALS
SLOWLY HOUR BY HOUR.

3. FORGOTTEN

THERE'S ALWAYS WAR THAT'S RAGING
SOMEWHERE IN THE WORLD,
PEOPLE DYING NEEDLESSLY
FROM BOMBS AND BULLETS HURLED.
AND SOMEWHERE THERE IS FAMINE,
SOMEONE DIES OF THIRST,
FEW THOUGHTS FOR THE NEEDY,
WE PUT THE FIGHTING FIRST.
I SIT AND WATCH THE EVENING NEWS
AND WHAT IS IT I SEE?
DEATH AND MORE DESTRUCTION,
AN AWFUL KILLING SPREE.
WE DO NOT SEE THE HUNGRY NOW
THE STRUGGLES THEY GO THROUGH,
THE ILLNESSES THEY SUFFER,
THE TEARS THAT THEY CRY TOO.
CAN'T WE PUT THE GUNS DOWN?
OUR DIFFERENCES ASIDE?
TRY AND HELP EACH OTHER,
WITH CARE, WITH LOVE, WITH PRIDE!

4. GAMES WE PLAY.

WHEN I WAS JUST A LITTLE BOY
WE PLAYED IN MANY WAYS,
COWBOYS, INJUNS, SOLDIERS
THROUGHOUT THE SUMMER DAYS.
AND WHEN WE KILLED EACH OTHER,
WE FELL DOWN ON THE FLOOR,
WE LAY QUITE STILL, ARMS OUTSTRETCHED
GOT UP TO FIGHT ONCE MORE.

AFTER MANY YEARS HAD PASSED
WE'D GONE OUR SEPARATE WAYS,
BUILDERS, PLUMBERS, SOLDIERS,
WAS HOW WE EARNED OUR PAY.
WHEN SOMEONE SHOT OUR PLAYMATE
HE FELL DOWN ON THE FLOOR,
HE LAY SO STILL AND LIFELESS
OUR FRIEND WOULD PLAY NO MORE.

AND AS WE LOOK BACK THROUGH THE YEARS
THOSE GAMES WE PLAYED BACK THEN,
BECAME A TRUE REALITY
WE'RE PLAYING ONCE AGAIN.
THE GUNS AND BULLETS NOW ARE REAL
AND I DON'T WANT TO PLAY,
I WANT TO LIVE MY LIFE IN PEACE
TOMORROW AND TODAY.

5. ?

HOW MANY STARS ARE IN THE SKY?
WHY DO CLOUDS GO DRIFTING BY?
WHAT STOPS THE SEA UPON THE SHORE?
DOES A BIRD EVER SNORE?
DOES A TREE EVER SLEEP?
HAVE YOU SEEN A FLOWER WEEP?
ALL THESE QUESTIONS AND SOME MORE
MAKE ME WONDER, WHAT LIFE'S FOR?

6. JOURNEY

THE BRIDGE SEEMED VERY NARROW
STRONG AND MADE OF STONE,
WHEN I STOOD THERE QUIETLY
THINKING ALL ALONE.
AND WATCHING WATER FLOWING BY
A SLOW AND LAZY STREAM
WHEN RIPPLES FROM A RAINDROP
AWOKE ME FROM MY DREAM.
WHERE I'D BEEN I SOON FORGOT
MY DREAM NOW WASHED AWAY,
BY THE FALLING RAINDROPS
THAT FELL ON ME THAT DAY.
I HEADED FOR SOME SHELTER
UNDERNEATH A TREE,
IT'S BRANCHES LOW AND LEAFY
SOON PROTECTED ME.
I STOOD THERE IN MY SHELTER
AND WATCHED THE FALLING RAIN,
THE RAINDROPS FALLING FROM THE LEAVES
TIME AND TIME AGAIN.
I STOOD AND WATCHED IN WONDER
THE MINUTES TICKING BY,
THE RAIN FELL MUCH MORE HEAVILY
FROM DARK CLOUDS IN THE SKY.
AND FORMING PUDDLES ON THE GROUND
NOT FAR FROM THE TREE
SLOWLY GROWING DRIP BY DROP
BUT NOT A DROP ON ME.
AWOKEN FROM MY DAYDREAMS
ONCE MORE I LOOKED AROUND
THE SKY WAS GETTING BRIGHTER
WHILE RAIN FELL TO THE GROUND.

JOURNEY. CONT.

AND WAY BEYOND THE BRANCHES
HIGH UP IN THE SKY
A RAINBOW SPREAD ITS COLOURS
TO WAVE THE RAIN GOODBYE.
I STEPPED OUT FROM MY SHELTER
AND STARTED ON MY WAY
ACROSS THE BRIDGE AND UP THE HILL
IN TO A SUNNY DAY.

7. FOUND TREASURES.

A FADED MEMORY
FROM A DUSTY PHOTOGRAPH,
OF SOMEONE THAT I USED TO KNOW
WHO REALLY MADE ME LAUGH,
SOMEONE WHO TOLD ME STORIES
FROM MANY YEARS AGO,
STORIES OF A LIFE WELL LIVED
OF SOMEONE THAT I KNOW.

A FADED MEMORY
FROM A LETTER IN A BOX,
HIDDEN IN A DRAWER
UNDERNEATH SOME SOCKS,
TELLING OF THE TALE
OF WHEN TWO PEOPLE MET,
TWO PEOPLE THAT I KNEW
AND NEVER WILL FORGET.

A FADED MEMORY
THAT'S NOW BROUGHT BACK TO LIFE
OF A VERY HAPPY COUPLE,
WHO BECAME A MAN AND WIFE,
THE MAN BECAME MY FATHER
MY MOTHER WAS HIS WIFE,
THAT DUSTY PHOTOGRAPH I FOUND
I'LL TREASURE ALL MY LIFE.

8. BERTIE.

I HAVE A GREAT BIG DOGGY
WHO REALLY LOVES ME SO,
HE LOOKS JUST LIKE A BALL OF FLUFF
GOES EVERYWHERE I GO.
HE LIKES TO SIT UPON MY KNEE
ALTHOUGH HE WEIGHS A LOT,
BUT WHEN I GET UP FROM MY CHAIR
HE QUICKLY FILLS MY SPOT.
HE LIKES TO GO OUT WALKIES
IN THE COUNTRY AIR,
IN THE SUN, OR IN THE RAIN
HE DOESN'T REALLY CARE.
HE LIKES TO HAVE HIS TUMMY RUBBED
AND WILL NOT LET ME GO,
FOR WHEN I STOP, HIS GREAT BIG PAW
WILL REALLY LET ME KNOW.
HE HITS ME HARD ACROSS THE KNEE
OR RIGHT UPON MY CHEST,
I HAVE TO KEEP ON RUBBING HIM
HE WILL NOT LET ME REST.
THERE'S ONE THING 'BOUT MY DOGGY
THAT I REALLY KNOW,
HE GIVES ME ALL THE LOVE HE HAS
THAT'S WHY I LOVE HIM SO.

9. IS IT JUST ME?
(OR AM I GROWING OLD?)

I THINK I MUST BE GROWING OLD
I JUST DON'T UNDERSTAND,
THE NEED FOR PEOPLE BREAKING LAWS
ALL ACROSS THE LAND.
WHAT'S THE POINT IN SPEEDING?
WHY TAKE A STUPID CHANCE?
PULLING OUT AT JUNCTIONS
WITHOUT A SECOND GLANCE.
WILL THEY GET THERE FASTER?
WHAT IS IT THEY GAIN?
AND YET THEY KEEP ON DOING IT
TIME AND TIME AGAIN.

I THINK I MUST BE GROWING OLD
I JUST DON'T UNDERSTAND
IN TODAY'S TECHNOLOGY
I NEED A GUIDING HAND.
TODAY I'M IN THE SAME PLACE
MY PARENTS USED TO BE
WITH VIDEO RECORDERS
IT'S SCARY NOW FOR ME.
I THINK I'M BEING LEFT BEHIND
AS THINGS MOVE ON SO FAST,
AS I BEGIN TO UNDERSTAND
THEY'RE OLD AND IN THE PAST.

IS IT JUST ME?
(OR AM I GROWING OLD?) CONT...

I THINK I MUST BE GROWING OLD
I JUST DON'T UNDERSTAND
THE NEED TO HAVE A MOBILE PHONE
ALWAYS IN THE HAND.
WHO IS IT THEY'RE CALLING
AND WHY CANNOT IT WAIT?
THEY'RE STARTING MAKING PHONE CALLS
BEFORE THEY LEAVE THE GATE!
ON THE PHONE WHILE SHOPPING
WHILE WALKING DOWN THE STREET
BUMPING IN TO PEOPLE
THEY HAVEN'T TIME TO GREET.

I THINK I MUST BE GROWING OLD
I JUST DON'T UNDERSTAND
MY JOINTS HAVE STARTED CREAKING
EVEN IN MY HAND,
I USED TO BE QUITE YOUTHFUL
RUSHING HERE AND THERE,
DOING LOT'S OF CRAZY THINGS
AND DIDN'T EVEN CARE.
NOW ALL I WANT TO DO AT NIGHT
IS HUDDLE IN MY CHAIR,
KEEPING MYSELF NICE AND WARM
OUT OF THE COLD NIGHT AIR.

10. MODERN MAN

SOME PEOPLE SEEM TO LOSE THEIR WAY
WHILST LIVING IN THE WORLD TODAY,
THEY DO NOT SEEM TO HAVE A CLUE
OF HOW TO BE OR WHAT TO DO,
THEY WANT IT ALL AND WANT IT NOW
DON'T EVEN ASK THE QUESTION "HOW?"

SOME PEOPLE TAKE BUT WILL NOT GIVE
IT'S HOW THEY SEEM TO ALWAYS LIVE,
THEY DO NOT EVEN SEEM TO CARE
AND DO NOT EVEN WANT TO SHARE,
THEY WANT THE BEST AND WANT IT NOW
I ASK THE QUESTION "WHY AND HOW?"

SOME PEOPLE LIVE A LIFE OF GREED
GET GIVEN EVERYTHING THEY NEED,
THEY DO NOT TAKE THE TIME TO THINK
BUT TAKE THE TIME TO SMOKE AND DRINK,
THEY GET THE BEST AND GET IT NOW
IT'S TIME WE ASKED THEM "WHY AND HOW?"

11. THINKING.

HERE I SIT WITH PEN IN HAND
I WATCH THE WORLD GO BY,
AND THINK ABOUT TOMORROW
WATCH CLOUDS UP IN THE SKY.
HERE I SIT ALL BY MYSELF
I FEEL A SUMMER BREEZE,
AND THINK ABOUT TOMORROW
WATCH BIRDS UP IN THE TREES.
HERE I SIT AND PONDER
I WATCH THE SETTING SUN,
AND THINK ABOUT TOMORROW
THINK OF WHAT'S TO COME.
HERE I SIT WITH PAD IN HAND
I WATCH THE WORDS UNFOLD,
AND THINK ABOUT TOMORROW
AND ALL THAT I'VE BEEN TOLD.
HERE I SIT WITH PEN IN HAND
WITH STORIES TO BE TOLD,
I SHOULD JUST THINK ABOUT TODAY
BEFORE I GET TOO OLD.

12. ESCAPE PLAN.

I SOMETIMES CAN'T BELIEVE MY EARS
OR THE THINGS I READ,
THIS WORLD THAT WE CALL CIVILIZED
SO FULL OF HATE AND GREED,
WITH PEOPLE SEEKING POWER
AND WANTING ALL CONTROL,
TELLING PEOPLE HOW TO BE
THEY'D STEAL YOUR VERY SOUL.
SOME PEOPLE DO NOT HAVE A CHOICE,
SOME PEOPLE ARE AFRAID,
OTHERS JUST ACCEPT THEIR LIVES
THE WAY THAT THEY ARE MADE.
AND IF SOMEBODY TRIES TO CHANGE
OR STEPS OUT OF THE LINE,
THEY PAY THE HIGHEST SACRIFICE
EVERY SINGLE TIME.
FOR SOME THE GRASS IS GREENER
ON THE OTHER SIDE,
THEY WANT TO MAKE THE GREAT ESCAPE
LIKE MANY OTHERS TRIED,
BUT SOME WILL NEVER MAKE IT,
THEY WILL NOT REACH THEIR GOAL,
THEY'LL BE RETURNED OR PUT IN JAIL,
OR BURIED IN A HOLE.

13. MANKIND

A DIFFERENT WAY OF LIVING
A DIFFERENT WAY TO DIE,
A DIFFERENT WAY OF LAUGHING
A DIFFERENT WAY TO CRY,
A DIFFERENT KIND OF PEOPLE
A DIFFERENT KIND OF NAME
WE'RE DIFFERENT ON THE OUTSIDE
BUT INSIDE ALL THE SAME.

14. LOYALTY

SO YOU THINK THAT HE'S CUTE CAUSE HE'S CUDDLY,
AND YOU THINK THAT HE'S CUTE WITH THOSE EYES,
WITH A NOSE THAT IS BLACK, WET AND SHINY
HE'S WEARING THE GREATEST DISGUISE!

HE CAN'T HIDE HIS ENERGY FROM YOU,
AND EVEN HIS MISCHIEVOUS WAYS,
HE'LL BEG FROM YOU WHILE YOU ARE EATING
WITH HIS BIG BROWN EYES AND HIS GAZE.

HE'LL JUMP IN YOUR CHAIR IF YOU STAND UP,
HE'LL PLAY WITH HIS TOYS WHILST YOU REST,
AND WHEN YOU ARE TIRED AND WEARY
YOU'LL STILL KNOW YOUR LIFE HAS BEEN BLESSED.

BLESSED BY A FRIEND TRUE AND LOYAL
WHO'LL STAY BY YOUR SIDE EVERY DAY,
HE'LL GIVE A LOVE UNCONDITION'L
IN HIS OWN LITTLE, SWEET DOGGY WAY.

15. WHERE ARE THEY NOW?

THE COUNTRY LANES I USED TO WALK
THE PEOPLE THAT I KNEW,
THE MANY BOOKS I LIKED TO READ
THE MUSIC LISTENED TO.
WHERE ARE THEY NOW?
WHERE HAVE THEY GONE?
JUST A MEMORY,
WHATEVER HAPPENED TO THEM?
AND WHAT WE USED TO BE.

THE HOUSES ALL AROUND ME
THE FIELDS, THE TREES, THE STREAMS,
ARE THEY IN MY FADING PAST?
OR WERE THEY JUST IN DREAMS?
WHERE ARE THEY NOW?
WHERE HAVE THEY GONE?
JUST A MEMORY,
WILL I EVER GO BACK?
WHAT WILL I GO TO SEE?

THE SOUNDS I USED TO LISTEN TO
THE SIGHTS I USED TO SEE,
PLACES THAT I VISITED,
IN TIMES THAT USED TO BE.
WHERE ARE THEY NOW?
WHERE HAVE THEY GONE?
JUST A MEMORY,
I'LL KEEP THEM NOW FOREVER
LOCKED INSIDE OF ME.

16. WHO, WHEN, WHY?

ON THE FAR HORIZON
IN THE FADING LIGHT
STANDS A LONELY FIGURE
ALMOST OUT OF SIGHT
STANDING THERE ALL ALONE
STANDING TALL AND PROUD
LOOKING OUT SILENTLY
LIKE SEARCHING THROUGH A CROWD
WHO KNOWS WHAT HE'S LOOKING FOR?
WHO KNOWS WHY SHE'S THERE?
HOW LONG HAVE THEY STOOD ALONE?
DO WE KNOW JUST WHERE?
IS IT JUST A FIGMENT?
OF SOMETHING IN MY MIND
IF I WALK UP TO THEM
WHO IS IT I'LL FIND?

17. BUT...

WE LIVE IN A WORLD
OF SUSPICION AND DOUBT
NEVER QUITE SURE
OF WHO'S OUT AND ABOUT,
NEVER QUITE SURE
OF WHAT'S GOING ON
AND THEN IT'S TOO LATE
WHEN SOMETHING GOES WRONG,
WE TRY TO BE TOLERANT
GIVE PEACE A CHANCE
BUT STILL THERE IS TROUBLE
WITH NO SECOND GLANCE.

WE LIVE IN A WORLD
OF TROUBLE AND STRIFE
WHERE NOBODY CARES
OF HOW THEY TREAT LIFE
NEVER QUITE SURE
OF WHO WE CAN TRUST
AND WHEN IT'S TOO LATE
WE FACE THE UNJUST,
WE TRY TO BE FAIR
AND NOT BE THE JUDGE
BUT STILL THERE ARE PEOPLE
HOLDING A GRUDGE.

BUT... (CONT)

WE LIVE IN A WORLD
OF VIOLENCE AND PAIN
FIGHTING AND KILLING
FOR GREED AND FOR GAIN
NEVER QUITE SURE
OF WHAT WE CAN DO
AND THEN IT'S TOO LATE
BUT NOTHING IS NEW,
WE TRY TO SHOW FAITH
IN ALL HUMANKIND
BUT ALWAYS LET DOWN
IN THE END, WE WILL FIND.

WE LIVE IN A WORLD
OF SUSPICION AND DOUBT
NEVER QUITE SURE
OF WHAT LIFE'S ABOUT
NEVER QUITE SURE
OF WHY WE GO ON
IS IT TOO LATE?
HAS THE WORLD ALL GONE WRONG?
WE TRIED TO BE TOLERANT
GAVE PEACE A CHANCE
BUT...

18. SPRINGTIME.

AS DARK CLOUDS GATHERED OVERHEAD
THE SUN BEGAN TO SHINE
A RAY OF HOPE WAS BEATING DOWN
WHICH MADE THE DAY FEEL FINE,
THE BIRDS WERE SINGING IN THE TREES
NOW SPRING WAS HERE ONCE MORE
THE WORLD WAS LOOKING GREAT AGAIN
JUST LIKE IT HAD BEFORE,
LEAVES WERE STARTING TO UNFURL
FLOWERS GAY AND BRIGHT
AND THOUGH THERE'S DARK CLOUDS OVERHEAD
THE WORLD'S A WONDROUS SIGHT.

19. THE WRONG QUEUE.

IS THERE SOME REASON
I ALWAYS GET
THE QUEUE THAT IS SLOWEST
I'M HELD UP AND YET
THE QUEUE WAS THE SHORTEST
ONE PERSON BEFORE
IT'S ALWAYS THE SAME
AND GETTING A BORE,
I'VE EVEN TRIED CHANGING
AND STILL IT'S THE SAME
IT FEELS LIKE SOMEONE
IS PLAYING A GAME,
THE QUEUE THAT I GO TO
COMES TO A HALT
THE QUEUE THAT I LEFT
MOVES WITHOUT FAULT,
WHY CAN'T I ONCE
JUST GO TO A QUEUE
WHERE NOTHING IS WRONG
AND MOVES SLOWLY THROUGH,
WHY SHOULD IT BE?
AND WHAT DID I DO?
TO ALWAYS BE IN
THE SLOW MOVING QUEUE?

20. THERE IS...

THERE'S SOMETHING STIRS MY SOUL
ON HEARING BIRDS THAT SING
EACH ONE SINGS A DIFFERENT TUNE
OH WHAT JOY THEY BRING,
MY HEART FEELS SO MUCH LIGHTER
ON WATCHING BUTTERFLY
EACH A BLAZE OF COLOUR
QUICKLY FLITTING BY,
THERE'S SOMETHING LIFTS MY SPIRIT
WHEN FLOWERS ARE IN BLOOM
AND LIFT'S IT SO MUCH HIGHER
ON SMELLING THEIR PERFUME,
MY HEART FEELS MUCH MORE HAPPY
I'M GLAD TO BE AROUND
WHEN SOMETHING STIRS MY SOUL
THAT'S NATURE – I HAVE FOUND.

21. WHO DECIDES?

WHO DECIDES MY DESTINY?
WHO DECIDES YOUR FATE?
AND WHO DECIDED YESTERDAY
TODAY WOULD BE TOO LATE?
TOMORROW SEEMS SO FAR AWAY
IN DREAMS FOR ME AND YOU,
IT SEEMS WE REALLY HAVE NO SAY
IN WHAT IT I WE DO.
WE THINK WE MAKE THE CHOICES
WHETHER RIGHT OR WRONG
BUT TAKE A LITTLE CLOSER LOOK
WHO CHOOSES ALL ALONG?

22. GROWING OLDER.

JUST LIKE MY DOG I'M GROWING OLD
THERE'S SOMETHING THAT HE SHOULD BE TOLD
I CAN'T PLAY GAMES OR RUN ABOUT
THAT'S SOMETHING WHICH IS SIMPLY OUT,
HE'LL LOOK AT ME WITH DOLEFUL EYE
A LOOK THAT MAKES ME WANT TO CRY
I HAVEN'T GOT THE ENERGY
TO RUN ABOUT NOW PLAYING FREE,
YET HE REMEMBERS DAYS OF OLD
WHEN WE WERE YOUNG AND FEELING BOLD
CHASING ROUND AND CATCHING STICK
NOW I'M SLOW BUT HE'S STILL QUICK
HE DOESN'T SEEM TO UNDERSTAND
WHY WE DON'T CHASE UPON THE SAND
HE'S STILL A FAITHFUL LOYA FRIEND
WE'LL STAY THAT WAY UNTIL THE END
AND THERE'S ONE THING WE BOTH CAN DO
LOVE EACH OTHER STRONG AND TRUE.

23. TRILOGY

1...

THE BIRDS WERE SUCH A PROBLEM
EATING ALL THAT GREW
LEFT WITHOUT AN OPTION
I HAD ONE THING TO DO,
I HAD A CAP, I HAD A SACK,
SOME CLOTHES I NEVER WORE.
I HAD SOME BOOTS, I HAD SOME GLOVES
AND LOTS AND LOTS OF STRAW,
I STUFFED THE TROUSERS AND THE SHIRT
PUT THE TWO TOGETHER
FILLED THE SACK AS MUCH I COULD
TOPPED WITH CAP AND FEATHER.
AT LAST THE GLOVES AND THEN THE BOOTS
I NEARLY WAS COMPLETE,
I MADE A FACE UPON THE SACK
SO NOW PLEASE WILL YOU MEET...(CONT)

2.
...MR SCARECROW TALL AND FAIR
I'M SURE YOU WILL AGREE
OF ALL THE SCARECROWS ALL AROUND
HE'S THE BEST YOU'LL SEE.
HE WON'T SAY "BOO!" TO ANYTHING
YET DOES HIS JOB REAL GRAND,
JUST STANDING THERE AND WATCHING
OVER ALL MY LAND.
NO LONGER HAVE I PROBLEMS
WITH BIRDS AND ALL THEIR GREED
THEY NOW GO IN TO NEXT DOORS GARDEN
WHEN THEY WANT A FEED.
MR SCARECROW TALL AND FAIR
IS SUCH A JOLLY CHAP
BUT NOW AND THEN I NOTICE
A ROBIN ON HIS CAP
HE'S OUT THERE IN ALL WEATHERS
IN WIND OR RAIN OR SHINE
AT TIMES HE'S LOOKING WEARY
AND YET HE'S DOING FINE.
I REALLY LIKE MY SCARECROW
HE'S SUCH A LOYAL FRIEND
HE GUARDS MY GARDEN VERY WELL
OUR FRIENDSHIP WILL NOT END.
AND MR SCARECROW TALL AND FAIR
HE'S BEEN HERE FOR A YEAR
I TALK TO HIM MOST EVERY DAY
I KNOW HE LENDS AN EAR,
HE LISTENS TO MY TALES OF WOE
AND NEVER ONCE COMPLAINS
AND JUST LIKE ME I'M SURE HE HAS
HIS LITTLE ACHES AND PAINS.
SOME PEOPLE THINK I'M CRAZY
OR JUST A LITTLE MAD
BUT MR SCARECROW IS FOR ME
THE BEST FRIEND I HAVE HAD. (CONT).

3.

I WENT TO BED LAST EVENING
THE WEATHER GETTING BAD
HEAVY WINDS AND LOTS OF RAIN
THE WORST THAT WE HAD HAD.
I LAY THERE IN MY BED AND SHIVERED
GLAD TO BE INSIDE,
BUT WHEN I ROSE THAT NEXT DAY
MY HEART SANK AND I CRIED.
THE SIGHT I SAW WAS HARD TO BEAR
NO MATTER HOW I TRIED
MR SCARECROW LAID OUT FLAT
I KNEW THAT HE HAD DIED,
I RAN INTO THE GARDEN
TO SEE WHAT I COULD DO
ALS MY FRIEND HAD PASSED AWAY
I HOPED THAT HE JUST KNEW,
HOW MUCH THAT HE HAD MEANT TO ME
AND JUST HOW MUCH I CARED,
SO THERE WS JUST ONE MORE THING TO DO
BECAUSE OF ALL WE'D SHARED...

THE END.

24. BEWARE!

TOMORROW SHOULD NOT BE DENIED
BY BULLET, BOMB OR KNIFE,
WE SHOULD NOT HAVE TO HIDE IN FEAR
OF WHO WILL TAKE OUR LIFE.
BUT EVERY DAY THERE SEEMS TO BE
THE SAME SAD SORRY TALE
OF SOME MORE LIVES THAT WERE CUT SHORT
WHERE DID MANKIND FAIL?
WE DO NOT LIVE IN HARMONY
AND DO NOT LIVE IN PEACE,
WE SEEM TO GO ON KILLING
IN WARS THAT NEVER CEASE.
AND IF IT ISN'T IN A WAR
WHERE SOMEONE ELSE IS KILLED
IT'S IN A PLACE WHICH ONCE FELT SAFE
THAT NOW GETS TERROR FILLED.
WILL OUR CHILDREN LIVE THEIR LIVES
FEARING WHAT'S TO COME
LOOKING ROUND IN TERROR
AND FEARING EVERYONE.
WE DO NOT SEE IT COMING
YET KNOW IT'S JUST OUT THERE
SOME WILL NOT ESCAPE IT
THOSE LEFT SHOULD JUST BEWARE!

25. IT MUST HAVE BEEN...PT 1.

IT MUST HAVE BEEN A MONDAY
I REMEMBER IT QUITE CLEAR
THE SUN WAS SHINING BRIGHTLY
AND SUMMERTIME WAS HERE,
WASHING LAID IN SEPARATE PILES
ALL ACROSS THE FLOOR
WHITES IN ONE PILE, COLOURS NEXT
WORK CLOTHES NEAR THE DOOR.
PILE BY PILE AND LOAD BY LOAD
THE WASHING SOON WAS DONE
HUNG OUT ON THE WASHING LINE
TO DRY OUT IN THE SUN.
A GENTLE BREEZE WOULD BLOW AROUND
STIRRING WHAT WAS HUNG
HELPING SPEED THE DRYING OF
THE ITEMS IN THE SUN,
EVERYTHING THEN WAS REMOVED
AS IT BECAME QUITE DRY
TAKEN BACK IN TO THE HOUSE
THE PILE SOON GREW QUITE HIGH,
CLOTHES THAT NEEDED PRESSING
WERE KEPT OUT SEPARATELY
READY TO BE IRONED
WHEN THE TIME WAS FREE,
THE REST WAS FOLDED NEATLY
AND QUICKLY PUT AWAY
WASHING DAY WAS OVER
UNTIL ANOTHER DAY.

26. IT MUST HAVE BEEN...PT 2.

IT MUST HAVE BEEN A TUESDAY
THE IRONING BOARD WAS OUT
AND CLOTHES THAT NEEDED PRESSING
WERE STILL LAID ALL ABOUT,
THE IRON STOOD UPON THE BOARD
ITS TEMPERATURE SOON ROSE
HEAT WAS COMING FROM IT
AS IT IRONED ALL THE CLOTHES
VERY QUICKLY PIECE BY PIECE
EVERYTHING WAS DONE
PRESSED AND FOLDED NEATLY
ITEMS ONE BY ONE.
THEN PLACED IN CUPBOARDS OR IN DRAWERS
THE CLOTHES WERE PUT AWAY
THE IRON LEFT TO STAND AND COOL
UNTIL ANOTHER DAY
THE IRONING BOARD WAS FOLDED UP
AND STORED BEHIND THE DOOR
THE WASHING BASKET EMPTY
PUT ON THE BATHROOM FLOOR,
READY TO BE FILLED AGAIN
WITH CLOTHES BOTH OLD AND NEW
ALL OF IT NOW DIRTY
NEEDED WASHING TOO.

27. IT MUST HAVE BEEN...PT 3.

IT MUST HAVE BEEN A WEDNESDAY
OF THAT I AM QUITE CLEAR
THE NOISE OF SOMEONE HOVERING
WAS SOUNDING IN MY EAR,
SCRAPPING OF THE FURNITURE
PUSHED ACROSS THE FLOOR
TO CLEAN AWAY THE DUST AND FLUFF
THAT GATHERED THERE ONCE MORE.
THINGS WERE LIFTED DOWN FROM SHELVES
POLISH SPRAYED AROUND
THE DUSTER RUBBED QUITE FRANTICALLY
WITHOUT A SINGLE SOUND.
EVERYWHERE SOON SPARKLED
SMELLING FRESH AND CLEAN
EVEN ALL THE WOODWORK
TOOK ON A BRAND NEW SHEEN.
WITH WATER IN A BUCKET
A CLOTH WITHIN ONE HAND
TO CLEAN THE WINDOWS OUTSIDE
AND MAKE THEM LOOK QUITE GRAND.
A HOUSEWIFE'S WORK WAS NEVER DONE
IT JUST WENT ON AND ON
FOR AS ONE JOB WAS FINISHED
ANOTHER HAD BEGUN.

28. IT MUST HAVE BEEN…PT 4

IT MUST HAVE BEEN A THURSDAY
I CAN'T REMEMBER WHY,
DID SOMETHING SPECIAL HAPPEN
OR DID IT JUST PASS BY?
I HAVE NO EXPLANATION
IT'S HOW IT SEEMED TO BE
NOTHING SPECIAL HAPPENED
THE DAY PASSED BY CAREFREE.
IT WASN'T LIKE THE OTHER DAYS
WHEN THINGS HAD TO BE DONE
YOU PLEASED YOURSELF ON THURSDAYS
THOSE DAYS ARE NOW LONG GONE.

29. IT MUST HAVE BEEN...PT5

IT MUST HAVE BEEN A FRIDAY
I REMEMBER IT QUITE WELL
PIES AND CAKES WERE BAKING
WHAT A LOVELY SMELL,
HOURS SPENT PREPARING
INGREDIENTS ALL LAID THERE
MIXING BOWLS, UTENSILS
NO ROOM WAS LEFT TO SPARE,
THE OVEN TURNED ON EARLY
READY FOR THE DAY
DIFFERENT SWEET AND SAVOURIES
LAID ALL OUT ON A TRAY,
EACH TRAY THAT WAS FULL OF FOOD
WAS QUICKLY PLACED WITHIN
AND ONCE IT FINISHED BAKING
WAS TAKEN FROM ITS TIN,
LAID UPON A COOLING RACK
COOLING PIECE BY PIECE
THE BAKING WENT ON THROUGH THE DAY
IT NEVER SEEMED TO CEASE,
CAKES AND JAM TARTS, NEW BAKED BREAD
DIFFERENT KINDS OF PIES
A WHOLE WEEKS WORTH OF BAKING
BEFORE OUR VERY EYES!

30. IT MUST HAVE BEEN... PT 6

IT MUST HAVE BEEN A SATURDAY
OF THAT I AM QUITE SURE
AS MOTHER WENT OUT SHOPPING
AT A LOCAL STORE,
GROCERIES FOR BUYING
FRUIT AND VEG AND MEAT,
SOMETIMES BOUGHT FROM MARKET STALLS
STANDING IN THE STREET,
CARRIED HOME IN SHOPPING BAGS
IT MUST HAVE WEIGHED A LOT,
WE WATCHED WITH EYES WIDE OPEN
TO SEE WHAT HAD BEEN BOUGHT,
BOX BY BOX AND BAG BY BAG
THINGS WERE STORED AWAY
A WHOLE WEEK'S WORTH OF GROCERIES
BOUGHT ON SHOPPING DAY.

31. IT MUST HAVE BEEN...PT 7

IT MUST HAVE BEEN A SUNDAY
SUPPOSED TO BE THE BEST
THE LAST DAY OF A BUSY WEEK
SHOULD BE A DAY OF REST,
BUT SOMEHOW THIS WAS NEVER SO
WITH PLENTY TO BE DONE
SUNDAY LUNCH SPENT COOKING
FOR EACH AND EVERYONE,
AND IF THE DAY WAS SUNNY
WARM AND VERY BRIGHT
A PICNIC TEA DOWN BY THE SEA
WOULD END THE DAY JUST RIGHT,
NO TIME OF REST FOR ANYONE
TO SIT AROUND AND LAZE
THERE STILL WAS LOTS OF THINGS TO DO
EVEN ON SUNDAYS,
IT MUST HAVE BEEN A WEEKDAY
OR WAS IT ONE WEEKEND?
I CANNOT QUITE REMEMBER HOW
MY MEMORIES SHOULD END.

32. SIMPLE THINGS.

I DIDN'T WANT TO CHANGE THE WORLD
OR BE A MOVIE STAR
I DIDN'T WANT A GREAT BIG HOUSE
OR DRIVE A REAL FAST CAR,
I'M NOT A MAN OF MONEY
MY WEALTH LIES DEEP WITHIN
I LIVE MY LIFE FROM DAY TO DAY
IT'S LIKE I ALWAYS WIN.

I DIDN'T WANT TO CATCH A STAR
FALLING FROM THE SKY
I WANTED JUST TO MAKE A WISH
WHILE WATCHING ONE PASS BY,
I'M NOT A MAN WHO WANTED MUCH
I STILL HAVE MUCH TO GIVE
DON'T TELL ME THAT IT'S VERY WRONG
THE WAY I WANT TO LIVE.

I DIDN'T WANT TO SAIL THE SEAS
OR TRAVEL FAR OFF LANDS
I LIKE TO PADDLE IN THE SEA
OR STROLL UPON THE SANDS,
I'M JUST A SIMPLE MAN AT HEART
WHO LIKES THE SIMPLE THINGS
I DO NOT LIKE THE COMPLICATIONS
MODERN LIFE NOW BRINGS.

I WANT TO HEAR THE SONG OF BIRDS
OR SEE THE FLOWERS GROW
I WANT TO WATCH A FLOWING STREAM
FEEL GENTLE BREEZES BLOW,
I'M JUST A SIMPLE MAN AT HEART
WHO LIKES THE SIMPLE WAY
DON'T TELL ME THAT IT'S VERY WRONG
TO LIVE FROM DAY TO DAY.

33. DEAF, DUMB AND BLIND.

ARE WE SO BUSY
WE JUST DO NOT SEE
THE KINDS OF THE THINGS
THAT HAPPEN 'ROUND "ME",
ARE WE SO OCCUPIED
SO DEAF AND BLIND
THAT IT TAKES A DISASTER
TO BRING IT TO MIND,
WE SEEM SO OBLIVIOUS
AND DON'T EVEN CARE
WE DON'T SEEM TO NOTICE
WHAT HAPPENS OUT THERE,
WE TURN A BLIND EYE
AND TURN A DEAF EAR
WE DON'T WANT TO SEE
WE DON'T WANT TO HEAR,
WE WON'T SPEAK OUT
WITH WHAT'S ON OUR MIND
KEEPING SO QUIET
WE'RE DEAF DUMB AND BLIND,
AND THOUGH OUR PATHS CROSS
WE DON'T EVER MEET
GOING ON DOWN
A ONE WAY STREET,
AND REACHING THE END
THERE'S NO GOING BACK
BUT ALL THAT WE NEED
IS THE COURAGE WE LACK.

34. EVERY DAY...ANOTHER DAY

EVERY DAY BY 8 O'CLOCK
HE'S BEEN OUT WITH SOME BREAD
STANDING BY THE POND SIDE
TO SEE THE DUCKS ARE FED.
EVERY DAY BY HALF PAST EIGHT
HE'S WALKED AWAY BACK HOME
MADE HIMSELF SOME BREAKFAST
AND PUT THE KETTLE ON.
EVERY DAY BY 10 AM
HE WALKS OUT OF THE DOOR
AND GOES DOWN TO THE LOCAL SHOP
OR TO A LOCAL STORE.
EVERY DAY BY LUNCHTIME
HIS PAPER HE HAS READ
THEN GOES IN TO HIS BEDROOM
AND LIES DOWN ON HIS BED.
EVERY DAY AT 3 O'CLOCK
HE MAKES HIMSELF A DRINK
AND HAS A CAKE OR SANDWICH
SITS AROUND TO THINK.
EVERY DAY BY 6 PM
THE DAY IS ALMOST DONE
HA HAS A LITTLE SUPPER
AND PUTS HIS NIGHT CLOTHES ON.
EVERY NIGHT BY 9 O'CLOCK
HE MAKES HIS WAY TO BED
ANOTHER DAY IS OVER
"ANOTHER DAY" HE SAID.

35. TO THE MEMORY OF THE FALLEN AND THE FUTURE OF THE LIVING.
NO MATTER –
WHEN THEY DIED OR WHERE THEY DIED
THOSE WARRIORS WERE SO BRAVE,
TO MARCH OUT INTO BATTLE
OUR FREEDOM, JUST TO SAVE.
NO MATTER –
HOW THEY DIED OR WHEN THEY DIED
THEY DID IT SELFLESSLY,
THEY MADE THEMSELVES A SACRIFICE
THEY DIED FOR YOU AND ME.
NO MATTER –
WHERE THEY DIED OR HOW THEY DIED
LET US NOT FORGET,
THE MEMORY OF THE FALLEN
TO THEM WE ARE IN DEBT.
NO MATTER –
WHO THEY ARE OR WHERE THEY ARE
MAY THEY KEEP SAFE AND WELL,
RETURN HOME TO THEIR FAMILIES
AND LIVE A LIFE TO TELL.
NO MATTER –
WHO THEY ARE OR WHERE THEY ARE
THEY DON'T KNOW YOU OR I,
BUT STILL THEY RISK THEIR LIVES FOR US
THEY RISK THAT THEY MIGHT DIE.
NO MATTER –
WHO THEY ARE OR WHERE THEY ARE
THEY FIGHT WITHOUT REGRET,
OUR FUTURES COULD BE IN THER HANDS
LET US NOT FORGET.
NO MATTER –
WHO THEY ARE OR WHEN THEY FOUGHT
LOOK THEM IN THE EYE,
GIVE THEM PRAISE AND GIVE THEM THANKS
AND NEVER PASS THEM BY.

36. MEMORY BOX.

DO YOU REMEMBER YEARS AGO
WHEN WE WERE VERY YOUNG?
THE BOOKS WE READ, THE GAMES WE PLAYED
THE SONGS THAT WE ALL SUNG.
NOT ALL HAD A TV SET
WE ALL HAD RADIO,
COMPUTERS WERE NOT HEARD OF
ALL THOSE YEARS AGO.
DO YOU REMEMBER YEARS AGO
BEFORE THE WORLD WENT MAD?
WE SEEMED TO BE MORE FRIENDLY
AND SEEMED TO BE LESS SAD.
THE NEWS WAS LESS SENSATIONAL
LIFE SEEMED MUCH MORE SLOW,
PEOPLE HAD MORE PATIENCE
ALL THOSE YEARS AGO.
DO YOU REMEMBER YEARS AGO
NOT MANY HAD A CAR?
WE TRAVELLED EVERYWHERE BY BUS
BE IT NEAR OR FAR.
AND IF WE HAD A HOLIDAY
THE COAST IS WHERE WE'D GO,
WE DIDN'T TRAVEL OVERSEAS
ALL THOSE YEARS AGO.
DO YOU REMEMBER YEARS AGO
OR HAVE YOU TOO FORGOT,
THE WINTERS SEEMED MUCH COLDER
THE SUMMERS MUCH MORE HOT.
AND AS THE WORLD GETS OLDER
MY AGE BEGINS TO SHOW
I CAN'T REMEMBER EVERYTHING
FROM ALL THOSE YEARS AGO!

37. YOUNG AT HEART

SOME PEOPLE SAY I'M YOUNG AT HEART
THAT ISN'T ALL THE TRUTH
FOR WHEN I LEFT MY TEENAGE YEARS
I TOOK WITH ME MY YOUTH
I'VE KEPT IT ALL THESE YEARS NOW
WHICH MAY SEEM RATHER STRANGE
I MAY BE GROWING OLDER
BUT DON'T INTEND TO CHANGE.
I'LL TRY AND BE RESPONSIBLE
AND DO THE THINGS I SHOULD
I'LL TRY AND DO SOME OTHER THINGS
IF ONLY I JUST COULD.
MY BODY MIGHT BE SLOWING DOWN
AS I AM GROWING OLD
BUT MY BRAIN KEEPS GOING JUST AS FAST
AND STILL REMAINS QUITE BOLD.
IT MAKES ME DO THE MANY THINGS
I KNOW I SHOULDN'T DO
THEY SAY THAT I AM YOUNG AT HEART
MY HEAD AND BRAIN IS TOO.

38. NIGHT RIDER

I GUESS WE ALL MIGHT DREAM ABOUT
A KNIGHT UPON A STEED
ONE TO WEAVE SOME MAGIC
INTO THE LIVES WE LEAD,
SOMEONE TO SWEEP US OFF OUR FEET
AND TAKE US FAR AWAY
TAKE US FROM THE ROUTINE CHORES
WE'RE DOING EVERY DAY,
SOMEONE BIG AND SOMEONE STRONG
AND SOMEONE WE DON'T KNOW
A HERO OF THE OLDEN STYLE
WHO ALWAYS SEEMED TO SHOW,
ARRIVING AT THE MOMENT
THE TIME YOU NEED HIM MOST
RIDING UP ON HORSEBACK
NO SHADOW OF A GHOST,
AND AS HE TAKES YOU IN HIS ARMS
YOU WAKE UP WITH A START
DISAPPOINTMENT IN YOUR EYES
A SIGH DEEP IN YOUR HEART.

39. TO LIVE AND BE FREE

I HOPE ONE DAY WE ALL FIND PEACE
AND LIVE IN HARMONY
NO NEED FOR SENSELESS KILLING
WHEN EVERYONE IS FREE.
A TIME TO LIVE AND LET LIVE
A TIME TO LOVE NOT HATE
NO LONGER LIVE OUR LIVES IN FEAR
WHEN WE DECIDE OUR FATE.

I HOPE ONE DAY WE ALL FIND LOVE
AND FRIENDSHIP ALL ABOUT
TO LIVE OUR LIVES THE WAY WE WANT
AND HAVE NO FEAR AND DOUBT.
A TIME TO LIVE TOGETHER
A TIME FOR PEACE NOT WAR
WHERE NATIONS DRAW TOGETHER
IN PEACE FOR EVER MORE.

40. I BELIEVE...

I DON'T BELIEVE THAT WHAT I SEE
WAS MADE BY CHANCE ALONE
HOW COULD BEAUTY THAT I SEE
DEVELOP ON ITS OWN.
THE TREES AND FLOWERS ALL ABOUT
THE GRASS UPON THE GROUND
SUCH VARIED COLOURS ALL ABOUT
WHEN I LOOK AROUND.

I CAN'T BELIEVE THAT WHAT I SEE
LIKE INSECTS BIRDS AND THINGS
WERE NOT CREATED LIKE THEY ARE
WITH EYES AND BEAKS AND WINGS.
THE ANIMALS UPON THE GROUND
THAT ROAM ACROSS THE EARTH
MUST HAVE BEEN CREATED
GIVEN LIFE AND BIRTH.

I CAN'T BELIEVE THAT WHAT I SEE
AND BEEN HERE ALL THESE YEARS
IS NOW BECOMING UNDER THREAT
WITH NO GRIEF OR TEARS.
WHY DOES MANKIND TEAR DOWN TREES
DESTROY SO THOUGHTLESSLY
FOR GREED WE KILL OFF NATURE
AND DO IT SELFISHLY.

I CAN'T BELIEVE THAT WHAT I SEE
WILL ONE DAY BE LONG GONE
THE SCENT OF FLOWERS IN THE AIR
THE MUSIC OF BIRD SONG.
ALL DESTROYED BY MANKIND
BECAUSE WE DO NOT CARE
WILL WE EVER MISS THESE THINGS
WHEN THEY'RE NO LONGER THERE?

41. ALL INNOCENCE.

DO YOU WANT TO SKIP AND SING
WHILE GOING DOWN THE STREET,
PULLING FACES, SAYING THINGS
TO STRANGERS THAT YOU MEET?
DO YOU WANT TO CLIMB A TREE
AND SIT THERE ALL DAY LONG,
OR FIND SOME LEAVES TO KICK AROUND
AND NOT FEEL THAT IT'S WRONG?
DO YOU WANT TO FIND SOME MUD
GET DIRTY AS CAN BE,
OR RING ON SOMEONE'S DOORBELL
THEN HIDE SO THEY CAN'T SEE?
DO YOU STILL CHASE BUTTERFLIES
CATCH TADPOLES IN A POOL,
PICK DAISIES IN A MEADOW
OR PLAY AND ACT THE FOOL?
CHILDHOOD DAYS OF INNOCENCE
TAUGHT US SUCH A LOT,
PERHAPS WE SHOULD REMIND OURSELVES
OF WHAT WE HAVE FORGOT.
THROW OUT INHIBITIONS
FIND WHAT WE ONCE HAD,
LET OURSELVES FEEL BETTER,
BE JOYFUL AND BE GLAD.

42. FRED 2

I HAVE A LITTLE SECRET
MY SECRET'S NAME IS FRED
HE'S BLACK AND HAIRY, HAS EIGHT LEGS
AND HIDES BENEATH MY BED.
SOMETIMES WHEN I AM FAST ASLEEP
HE CRAWLS INSIDE WITH ME
GETS RIGHT BENEATH THE COVERS
JUST WHERE I CANNOT SEE.
I SOMETIMES FEEL HIM MOVING
AS HE CRAWLS ACROSS MY CHEST
I REALLY DON'T LIKE SPIDERS
AND HE PUTS ME TO THE TEST.
I WANT TO SCREAM AND SQUASH HIM
BUT KNOW THAT I CANNOT
I BRAVELY LAY THERE MOTIONLESS
WITH ALL THE STRENGTH I'VE GOT.
I'M SURE MY SPIDER LIKES ME
OR IS HE JUST A TEASE?
DOES HE WANT TO SCARE ME
OR TRYING JUST TO PLEASE?
I REALLY DON'T LIKE SPIDERS
BUT TOLERATE MY FRED
I ONLY WISH I DIDN'T KNOW
WHEN HE WAS IN MY BED!

43. SOMETHING FOR NOTHING – IT'S FREE!

WHAT BEAUTY AND WHAT WONDER
IN THE EARLY MORNING LIGHT
THE SUN ON THE HORIZON
JUST COMING INTO SIGHT,
A GENTLE BREEZE IS BLOWING
AND RUSTLING THROUGH A TREE
THERE'S BEAUTY AND THERE'S WONDER
IN EVERYTHING I SEE,
WHAT BEAUTY AND WHAT WONDER
IN EARLY BIRDS THAT SING
THEY BREAK THE EARLY MORNING PEACE
AS THEY ARE ON THE WING
NOTHING ELSE IS STIRRING
OR EVEN MAKES A SOUND
THERE'S BEAUTY AND THERE'S WONDER
EVERYWHERE AROUND,
WHAT BEAUTY AND WHAT WONDER
TO AMAZE AND TO ASTOUND
ALL ABOUT AND EVERYWHERE
JUST WAITING TO BE FOUND
TAKE THE TIME TO NOTICE
THOSE LITTLE THINGS I SEE
THE BEAUTY AND THE WONDER
AND ALL OF IT IS FREE!

44. DO YOU KNOW WHERE YOU'RE GOING TO?

DO NOT ASK I DO NOT KNOW
AND DO I REALLY CARE?
I'LL FOLLOW MY NOSE STRAIGHT AHEAD
TO WHO KNOWS WHAT OR WHERE?
AM I LOST OR AM I FOUND
WHERE HAVE I REALLY BEEN?
I'LL JUST KEEP MOVING FORWARD
THROUGH THIS LOVELY SCENE.
DO I KNOW OR DO I CARE
OR DOES IT WORRY ME?
WHERE I AM AND WHERE I'M GOING
I'M HERE AND I AM FREE.
DO NOT ASK I DO NOT KNOW
I DO NOT REALLY CARE
AS LONG AS I AM HAPPY
ON THE ROAD TO ANYWHERE.

45. YOUR MAJESTY.

OLD AND GNARLED NOT WRINKLED
YOU STAND SO REGALLY
NOT SURROUNDED – ON YOUR OWN
SO EVERYONE CAN SEE.
DOES ANYBODY NOTICE YOU
OR DO THEY WALK ON PAST?
STANDING THERE A LONG TIME NOW
WHEN LOT'S OF TIME HAS PASSED.
YOU'RE THERE IN EVERY WEATHER
IN SUN OR RAIN OR SNOW
YOU EVEN KEEP ON STANDING THERE
WHEN HEAVY WINDS DO BLOW.
YOU RAISE YOUR ARMS IN SPLENDOUR
I CALL YOU "MAJESTY"
I BOW MY HEAD OR RAISE MY HAT
TO YOU THE "GREAT OAK TREE"!

46. ANOTHER DAY

I HAVE WALKED A COUNTRY LANE
AND SEEN THE GOLDEN CORN
SURROUNDED BY A HEDGEROW
ON A BRIGHT AND JOYOUS MORN,
I HAVE SEEN THE RABBITS
IN THE EARLY MORNING SUN
DARTING HERE, DASHING THERE
PLAYING, HAVING FUN,
I HAVE WATCHED A HERD OF COWS
GRAZING PEACEFULLY
STANDING UP OR LYING DOWN
SLOW AND SO CAREFREE,
I HAVE HEARD THE MORNING BIRDS
SINGING IN A TREE
I THANK THE LORD FOR ONE MORE DAY
AND GIVING THIS TO ME.

47. A WISH...

I WISH I COULD PACK UP
A SUITCASE OF SUNSHINE
AND BRING IT BACK HOME WITH ME...

I WISH I COULD SWEEP UP
THE DARK CLOUDS ABOVE
AND PUSH THEM INTO THE SEA...

I WISH I COULD PICK UP
THE SPARKLE AND GLITTER
FROM STARS THAT SHINE IN THE NIGHT...

I WISH I COULD SHARE OUT
THE LOVE AND THE LAUGHTER
AND TURN ALL THE WRONG THINGS RIGHT.

48. A WINTER LOVE STORY.

SHE FELL ASLEEP
NO MORE AWAKE
UPON THAT CHILLY MORN,
THE COLD WINDS BLEW
AROUND THE HILLS
UPON IT SNOW WAS BORNE.

THE SNOW IT FELL
SO HARD AND FAST
UPON THE OPEN GROUND,
IT COVERED EVERYWHERE
IN WHITE
WITHOUT A SINGLE SOUND.

SILENTLY THE NIGHT
IT CAME
A CLOAK ACROSS THE LAND,
THEN STARS BEGAN
TO TWINKLE
WITH MOONBEAMS HAND IN HAND.

HAND IN HAND
THEY WANDERED
THROUGH THE FALLING SNOW,
TWO YOUNG PEOPLE
SO IN LOVE
WITH NOWHERE ELSE TO GO.

AND NOWHERE
COULD BE BETTER
THAN WALKING THROUGH THE SNOW,
UNTIL THE MOON
FALLS FAST ASLEEP
AND STARS NO LONGER SHOW.

49. TONIGHT, TONIGHT AND EVERY NIGHT.

HOW SILENTLY THE NIGHT TIME FALLS
AND CREEPS ACROSS THE LANDS
HOW GENTLE ARE THE NIGHT BIRD CALLS
AS DARKNESS NOW DESCENDS
AND AS THE CLOUDS ARE PARTING
THE MOON BEGINS TO SHINE
THE DAYLIGHT ONCE DEPARTING
A MEMORY IN TIME
THE TWINKLING OF THE STARLIGHT
ADDS MAGIC TO THE SKY
A WORLD NOW HIDDEN OUT OF SIGHT
AND BREEZES HEAVE A SIGH
WITH QUIET AND A TRANQUIL PEACE
THE WORLD SEEMS MUCH MORE CALM
AND TROUBLES, WORRIES SEEM TO CEASE
THE WORLD FEELS FREE FROM HARM
TONIGHT, TONIGHT AND EVERY NIGHT
A HAVEN FOR THE WORLD
LIKE PETALS OF A FLOWER
PEACE IS NOW UNFURLED.

50. CHANGES

A SUMMER SUN
A WINTER MOON
A STORMY AUTUMN AFTERNOON
A SPRINGTIME SHOWER
TO SOAK US THROUGH
SEASONS CHANGE THE SCENIC VIEW.

A CLOUDY SKY
A FROSTY NIGHT
A FOG THAT HIDES THE WORLD FROM SIGHT
THE COLDEST DAY
THAT SOON BRINGS SNOW
SEASONS CHANGE AND COME AND GO.

THE COLD OF NIGHT
THE HEAT OF DAY
EACH ONE CHASE EACH ONE AWAY
SEASONS COME
AND SEASONS GO
EACH ONE CHANGING WHAT WE KNOW.

51. WHAT WE DID...

CHILD OF THE COUNTRY –

RAN THROUGH MEADOWS, CLIMBED UP TREES
SPLASHED IN PUDDLES
GRAZED BOTH KNEES
KICKED THROUGH LEAVES, FISHED IN STREAMS
ROLLED DOWN HILLS
LIVED OUT DREAMS.

CHILD OF THE COUNTRY –

PLAYED IN SNOW, PLAYED IN RAIN
HID FROM THUNDER
LAUGHED AT PAIN
WALKED A LANE, CLIMBED A GATE
PLAYED OUTSIDE
OUT 'TIL LATE.

CHILD OF THE COUNTRY –

WATCHING BIRDS, WILDLIFE TOO
DID ALL THIS
BUT THEN WE GREW
WE HAD NO WORRIES, HAD NO FEAR
WE LIVED OUR LIVES
FROM YEAR TO YEAR.

52. AS YEARS GO BY.

SHE LOOKED IN HER MIRROR
AND WHAT DID SHE SEE?
IT WASN'T THE WOMAN
SHE DREAMED SHE WOULD BE.
OLDER AND WISER,
AS YEARS GO BY
SHE LOOKED HERSELF,
STRAIGHT IN THE EYE.
"WHERE AM I GOING?
AND WHERE HAVE I BEEN?
WHAT HAVE I HEARD?
AND WHAT HAVE I SEEN?"

HE SAW HIS REFLECTION
WHAT WAS IT HE SAW?
A FACE FULL OF LIFE
AND SO MUCH MORE.
OLDER AND WISER,
THROUGH GATHERING YEARS
HE SAW HIMSELF,
HIS WORRIES HIS FEARS.
"WHAT AM I DOING?
AND WHAT HAVE I DONE?
A WIFE AND A DAUGHTER
A GROWN UP SON."

THEY SAW THEIR IMAGES
WHAT DID THEY SEE?
TWO HAPPY PEOPLE
QUITE HAPPY AND FREE.
OLDER AND WISER,
THAN WHEN THEY BEGAN,
THEY SAW THEMSELVES
A WOMAN, A MAN.
"WHERE ARE WE GOING?"
THEY ASK THEMSELVES "WHY?"
WITH ALL THAT THEY'VE DONE
AS YEARS GO BY.

53. FAMILY TREE.

I KNOW YOUR NAME, I KNOW YOUR AGE
AND EVEN WHERE YOU'RE FROM
BUT THROUGH THE PASSING AGES
YOU'RE STORY IS NOW GONE
THE FATHERS OF MY FATHERS, FATHERS
FALLING BACK THROUGH TIME
YOU CAME, YOU WENT BEFORE ME
YET GAVE TO ME WHAT'S MINE
I DON'T KNOW MUCH ABOUT YOU
WHICH REMAINS A MYSTERY
DO WE SHARE SOME QUALITIES
ARE YOU PART OF ME?
IF I COULD TAKE A STEP IN TIME
AND TAKE A LOOK AT YOU
WOULD I BE LOOKING BACK AT ME
OR SOMEONE ELSE QUITE NEW?
ARE WE VERY SIMILAR
IN WHAT WE DO OR SAY?
AND DO I CARRY IN ME
A PART OF YOU TODAY?

54. MY TOWN

RUN DOWN SHOPS
ON A DEAD END STREET
THE BAR NOW CLOSED
WHERE ONCE WE'D MEET
THE PAVEMENT CRACKED
FROM DISREPAIR
MY TOWN CRIES OUT
IN SAD DESPAIR
NO ONE COMES HERE
ANY MORE
WHAT IS LEFT
TO COME HERE FOR?
THE SHOPS ALL MOVED
TO OUT OF TOWN
THE CENTRE DIED
AND JUST CLOSED DOWN
IT COULD NOT LIVE
COULD NOT SURVIVE
WE COULD NOT KEEP
MY TOWN ALIVE
WITHOUT A HEART
WITHOUT A SOUL
MY TOWN NO LONGER
HAS A GOAL
IT'S SAD TO THINK
THEY'LL TEAR IT DOWN
AND JUST BUILD HOUSES
ON MY TOWN.

55. LONG MAY IT CONTINUE.

A PATCHWORK QUILT
OF FIELDS AND FENCE
FIELDS AND HEDGE, FIELDS AND WALL
ENCLOSING MUCH OF GOD'S CREATION
WINTER, SPRING
SUMMER, FALL.

A PATCHWORK QUILT
OF TREES AND BUSHES
FIELDS OF COWS, FIELDS OF SHEEP
ALL OF WHICH IS GOD'S CREATION
EATING, DRINKING
FAST ASLEEP.

A PATCHWORK QUILT
OF PLOUGHED OR GRASS LAND
FIELDS OF BEAST OR FIELDS OF CROP
ALL OF WHICH ARE GODS CREATION
MAY THEY GROW
AND NEVER STOP.

56. GOING, GOING ALMOST GONE...

A BROKEN DOWN SHED
WITH A BROKEN DOWN DOOR
THE WINDOW LONG GONE
AND THERE'S MUD FOR A FLOOR
THE SHED LONG FORGOTTEN
SURROUNDED BY TREE
AND JUST A FEW POSTS
WHERE A FENCE USED TO BE
THE ROOF HAS COLLAPSED
AND LAYS ALL ABOUT
NO ONE COMES HERE NOW
THE LIGHTS ARE ALL OUT
THE UNDERGROWTH GROWING
AND BLOCKING THE WAY
NO ONE'S BEEN HERE
FOR MANY LONG DAY
A SHED THAT WAS ONCE USED
BY FARMER AND WIFE
SLOWLY FALLS DOWN
AT THE END OF ITS LIFE.

57. FORGET ME NOTS

THE SMILE SHOWS RECOGNITION
OF SOMEONE THAT HE KNOWS
THE LOOK OF SADNESS IN HIS EYES
IS WHAT HIS HEART NOW SHOWS
THE FEAR OF WHAT IS HAPPENING
THE THINGS THAT HE WILL LOSE
ALL THE THINGS THAT HE WILL MISS
YOU CANNOT PICK AND CHOOSE
IT CREPT UP VERY SLOWLY
AND TOOK HOLD OF HIS MIND
LEAVING HIM NO FUTURE
OR PAST HE LEFT BEHIND
HE KNOWS YOU CAN'T CONTROL IT
IT TAKES CONTROL OF YOU
ROBBING YOU OF ALL YOU HAD
RESTRICTING ALL YOU DO
AND AS IT TAKES CONTROL OF HIM
HE KNOW'S WHAT'S GOING ON
TAKING ALL HIS MEMORIES
THE LIFE THAT WAS, THEN GONE
SOMEDAYS HE CAN REMEMBER
AND OTHER DAYS CANNOT
HE'LL JUST SIT IN A CORNER
HIS MEMORIES FORGOT.

58. THE CREEPER.

I DON'T WANT TO MOAN ABOUT AGEING
BUT IT'S SOMETHING COMING MY WAY
CREEPING UP ON ME SLOWLY
EACH AND EVERY DAY
I NOTICED IT FIRST WITH THE CREAKING
AND THEN WITH THE ACHES IN MY JOINTS
MY HEARING IS SLOWLY FADING
JUST ONE OR TWO OF THE POINTS
MY APPETITE AIN'T WHAT IT ONCE WAS
MY TEETH ARE WEARING AWAY
THE HAIR ON MY HEAD IS RECEDING
AND TURNING A BRIGHT SHADE OF GREY.
I FIND I WANT TO START SLEEPING
EACH TIME I SIT IN MY CHAIR
I PUT DOWN THE KEYS A MOMENT AGO
BUT CANNOT REMEMBER JUST WHERE
I WILL NOT SAY OLDER AND WISER
THERE'S LESSONS I LEARN EVERY DAY
AS LONG AS I HOLD TO MY DIGNITY
I'LL GROW OLD IN MY OWN WAY.

59. A CRY : A PLEA

A CRY IN THE DARKNESS
FOR SOMEONE TO CARE
WILL ANYONE LISTEN?
IS ANYONE THERE?
A CRY FROM THE HEART
A PITIFUL PLEA
WILL ANYONE LISTEN?
WILL ANYONE SEE?
A CRY OUT IN PAIN
FROM HURT AND ABUSE
WILL ANY LISTEN?
OR IS IT NO USE?
A CRY IN DISTRESS
ONE OF DESPAIR
DOES NOBODY LISTEN?
DOES NOBODY CARE?

60. THE APPROACH

THE MIST THAT ROLLS ACROSS THE LAND
AND FROST UPON THE GLASS
ARE SIGNS OF WINTER FAST APPROACHING
SUMMER NOW HAS PASSED
BREATH THAT RISES IN THE AIR
A SHIVER FROM A CHILL
NATURE STARTS TO GO TO SLEEP
AND ALL ABOUT IS STILL
THE SUMMER FLOWERS DYING
SLOWLY ONE BY ONE
THE LEAVES ARE TURNING GREEN TO GOLD
THE BUTTERFLIES HAVE GONE
THE DAYS ARE GROWING SHORTER NOW
THE NIGHTS SEEM MUCH MORE DARK
LOGS ARE BURNING IN THE GRATE
AND GIVING OFF A SPARK
IT'S TIME TO CURL UP IN A CHAIR
AND WRAP UP WARM AND NICE
AS WINTER FAST APPROACHES
WITH WINDS AND SNOW AND ICE.

61. HOME.

I HAVE TRAVELLED ROUND A LOT
AND BEEN TO MANY PLACES
SEEN A LOT OF CHEERY SMILES
ON VERY MANY FACES
I'VE EVEN SHARED SOME SADNESS
WITH PEOPLE THAT I KNOW
I HAVE EVEN SHARED THEIR JOY
AND WATCHED OUR FRIENDSHIP GROW
I'VE SAT ALONE AT HOME AT NIGHT
AND WATCHED THE HOURS GO BY
SAT AND TALKED FOR HOURS AND HOURS
WATCHED CLOUDS IN THE SKY
I HAVE HAD SO MANY DREAMS
AND HAD A LOT OF FEARS
I HAVE HAD A LOT OF LAUGHTER
HAD MY SHARE OF TEARS
IT DOESN'T MATTER WHERE I GO
OR EVEN WHERE I ROAM
WHAT THEY SAY IS VERY TRUE
THERE IS NO PLACE LIKE HOME.

62. ANOTHER SIDE

WHAT HAPPENED TO THE LADY
WHO USED TO LIVE NEXT DOOR
SHE COULD BE PRIM AND PROPER
AND REALLY QUITE A BORE
WE NEVER QUITE SAW EYE TO EYE
WE'D SOMETIMES DISAGREE
WE NEVER REALLY ARGUED
WE LET EACH OTHER BE
THEN ONE DAY SOMETHING HAPPENED
THEY TOOK HER TO A HOME
I HAD TO GO AND VISIT
AS I KNEW SHE WAS ALONE
THIS THING HAD CREPT UPON HER
THE CHANGE HAD BEEN QUITE SLOW
HER MEMORIES HAD ALL GONE NOW
SHE HAD NOWHERE TO GO
ON SOME DAYS SHE IS HAPPY
AND SOME DAYS SHE IS SAD
BUT NOW SHE GETS TO LEAD THE LIFE
THAT SHE NEVER HAD
SHE LAUGHS AT ALL THE JOKES WE TELL
AND LIKES TO WATCH TV
AND SOMETIMES IF I GET TOO CLOSE
SHE'LL PLACE A KISS ON ME!
THE CHANGE THAT CAME UPON HER
IS SUCH A JOY TO SEE
ALTHOUGH HER LIFE HAS CHANGED A LOT
SHE'S HAPPY AND CAREFREE!

63. AUTOBIOGRAPHY

YOU ARE THE FUTURE OF MY HISTORY
AS I AM GROWING OLD
THE STORY FROM MY YOUNGER DAYS
WAITING TO BE TOLD
WITH TALES TO MAKE YOU SMILE OUT LOUD
AND SOME TO MAKE YOU THINK
A NUDGE, A NOD "I TOLD YOU SO!"
OR JUST A SINGLE WINK
STORIES MADE FOR SHARING
AND SECRETS TO BE TOLD
READY TO BE WROTE ABOUT
NOW I AM GROWING OLD
REMEMBERING THE FUTURE
AND THE DAYS OF MY LIVED PAST
THE PAGES TURNING ONE BY ONE
MY STORY TOLD AT LAST.

64. LONG FORGOTTEN HERO

A PILLOW MADE FROM CONCRETE
A BLANKET MADE OF CARD
LIVING HOMELESS ON THE STREETS
LIFE CAN BE SO HARD.
EATING FROM A DUSTBIN
DISCARDED, BOTTLED, DRINK
HOW DO WE LET THIS HAPPEN?
AND HOW LOW DO WE SINK?
SOMETIMES THERE'S PEOPLE GIVE THEIR ALL
YOU DON'T HEAR THEM COMPLAIN
WHY WE LET THEM GET SO DOWN
CAN ANYONE EXPLAIN?
AND WHO WILL GIVE THEM COMFORT
NOT JUST PASS THEM BY?
LISTEN TO THEIR STORY
AND ASK THE QUESTION WHY?
A LONG FORGOTTEN HERO
SHOULD LEAD A LIFE LIKE THIS
INSTEAD OF BEING CARED FOR
THERE'S SOMETHING NOW AMISS.

65. AUTUMN LEAVES A MEMORY.

KICKING THROUGH THE FALLEN LEAVES
THAT RUSTLE NEATH MY FEET
BRINGS BACK CHILDHOOD MEMORIES
OF RUNNING DOWN THE STREET
A DARKENED VILLAGE THOROUGHFARE
WITH TREES NOW TURNING GOLD
FALLING LEAVES LIKE RAINDROPS
AS THE YEAR GROWS OLD
MEMORIES HOW WE'D KICK THE LEAVES
OR PUSH THEM IN TO PILES
THEN RUN AND JUMP IN TO THEM
WITH LAUGHTER AND WITH SMILES
AND AS THEY BLEW AROUND OUR FEET
WE LIKED TO KICK OUR WAY
WE DIDN'T MIND THE WEATHER
OR THE TIME OF DAY
AND GATHERED FOR A BONFIRE
THE LEAVES WERE PILED UP HIGH
THEY ALWAYS TOOK A WHILE TO BURN
ALTHOUGH THEY WERE QUITE DRY
AND NOW I AM AN OLDER MAN
I STILL WILL KICK MY FEET
THROUGH THE NEWLY FALLEN LEAVES
LYING IN THE STREET.

66. DO YOU REMEMBER...?

DID YOU GROW UP WITH ANDY PANDY
LOOBY LOO AND TED?
AND DID YOU ALWAYS BRUSH YOUR TEETH
BEFORE YOU WENT TO BED?
BLUE PETER OR MAGPIE
WHICH ONE WAS FOR YOU?
CRACKERJACK ON FRIDAY
ESSENTIAL THINGS TO VIEW
HOMEWORK DONE BY BEDTIME
TWO CHANNELS ON T.V.
OR LISTENED TO A WIRELESS
ONCE YOU HAD YOUR TEA
PROGRAMMES SHOWN IN BLACK AND WHITE
THE TEST CARD IN THE DAY
YOU DIDN'T HAVE TO STAY INDOORS
WHEN YOU WENT TO PLAY
PENNY CHEWS AND LOLLIPOPS
WHICH ONE DID YOU PICK?
YOU'D EAT A LOT OF CHOCOLATE
AND MAKE YOURSELF FEEL SICK!
DID YOU HAVE A PUSSYCAT?
OR DID YOU HAVE A DOG?
OR DID YOU CAPTURE CREEPY CRAWLIES
UNDERNEATH A LOG?
MEMORIES OF YOUNGER DAYS
OF TIMES THAT HAVE NOW GONE
CHILDHOOD DAYS HAVE CHANGED SO MUCH
DO CHILDREN STILL HAVE FUN?
THE KIND OF FUN THAT WE HAD
WITH ALL THE THINGS WE'D DO
A SHAME THAT THEY ARE MISSING OUT
ON EVERYTHING WE KNEW.

67. TRAVELS IN MY LIFE.

HOW LITTLE THAT WE WERE
SO LITTLE DID WE KNOW
THAT AS WE KEPT ON GROWING
JUST HOW FAR WE WOULD GO.
FROM PUSHCHAIRS IN OUR CHILDHOOD
WE CLIMBED ON TO OUR FEET
THE WORLD CHANGED FROM OUR GARDENS
AND OUT IN TO THE STREET.
WE SLOWLY GREW AND CHANGED A LOT
FROM BICYCLE TO CAR
OUR WORLD WAS CHANGING CONSTANTLY
WE TRAVELLED NEAR AND FAR.
THE WORLD WAS SLOWLY SHRINKING
AND AS WE SPREAD OUR WINGS
OUR HOMELAND GREW TOO SMALL FOR US
WE WANTED GREATER THINGS.
WE CLIMBED ON TO A SHIP OR BOAT
WE GOT IN TO A PLANE
CROSSED THE OCEANS DEEP AND WIDE
TIME AND TIME AGAIN.
AND EACH TIME THAT WE TRAVELLED
THE FURTHER WE WOULD GO
UNTIL WE'D TRAVELLED EVERYWHERE
IN SUN AND RAIN AND SNOW.
NOW AS WE GET MUCH OLDER
HOW FAST WE SOON SLOW DOWN
THE WIDE WORLD SHRINKS BEHIND US
OUR WORLD IS NOW OUR TOWN.

68. HEARTBREAK EXPRESS
(FOR DAVID)

THE TRAIN PULLED IN
AND YOU GOT ON
AND ALL TOO SOON
THE TRAIN WAS GONE
AND YOU WOULD NOT RETURN

NO STATION AND NO PLATFORM
A TRAIN JUST FULL OF LOVE
HEADED FOR ETERNITY
AND ALWAYS ON THE MOVE.

**FORGET ME NOT
FOR WHEN I'M GONE
MY MEMORY
WILL STILL LIVE ON
FORGET ME NOT
THROUGHOUT THE COMING DAYS**

**FORGET ME NOT
FOR WHEN I'M GONE
MY MEMORY
WILL STILL LIVE ON
FORGET ME NOT
THROUGHOUT THE COMING YEARS**

I MET YOU HERE
WHEN YOU FIRST CAME
THE START OF LIFE
WAS JUST A GAME
AND ON AND ON WE WENT

NO TIME FOR US TO STOP AND STARE
WE JUST KEPT GOING ON
HEADED FOR THE FUTURE
OUR PAST WAS SOON LONG GONE

HEARTBREAK EXPRESS (Cont.)

**FORGET ME NOT
FOR WHEN I'M GONE
MY MEMORY
WILL STILL LIVE ON
FORGET ME NOT
THROUGHOUT YOUR WHOLE LIFE LONG**

**FORGET ME NOT
FOR WHEN I'M GONE
MY MEMORY
WILL STILL LIVE ON
FORGET ME NOT
UNTIL YOUR DYING DAY**

THE TRAIN PULLED IN
AND YOU GOT ON
YOU DIDN'T SEEM TO MIND
THE TRAIN PULLED OUT
I SHED A TEAR
NOW I AM LEFT BEHIND

**FORGET US NOT
FOR WHEN WE'RE GONE
OUR MEMORIES
WILL STILL LIVE ON
FORGET US NOT
THROUGHOUT THE FUTURE DAYS.**

69. DON'T ASK...I DIDN'T

MY LIFE IS PART OF HISTORY
AS I AM GROWING OLD
LIVING THROUGH THE HAPPENINGS
IN STORIES THAT ARE TOLD.
CHANGES HAPPEN YEAR TO YEAR
LITTLE STAYS THE SAME
AND LIFE IS JUST A MYSTERY
IN EVERYTHING BUT NAME.
I'VE SEEN A MAN WALK ON THE MOON
AND LISTEN TO THE STARS
I'VE SEEN HIM BUILDING BIGGER
AND FASTER PLANES AND CARS.
I'VE SEEN AS MEN GO OFF TO WAR
TO KILL HIS FELLOW MAN
I'VE SEEN A DOCTOR FIGHT FOR LIFE
AND SAVE IT IF HE CAN.
I'VE WONDERED WHAT IT'S ALL ABOUT
AND WHERE WHERE HEADED TO
OUR LIVES ARE PART OF HISTORY
AND YET WE NEVER KNEW.

70. TRUST

WHY ARE WE SO ANGRY
AND WHY DO WE GET MAD?
DOES NOBODY REMEMBER
ABOUT THE LOVE WE HAD?
A LOVE FOR ONE ANOTHER
WHEN EVERYBODY CARED
AND PEOPLE SEEMED MORE HAPPY
AND EVERYBODY SHARED.
WHAT IS ALL THE RUSH ABOUT
TO GET FROM A TO B
NO ONE WANTS TO TAKE THEIR TIME
THEY DO NOT GET TO SEE
TELL ME WHAT HAS HAPPENED
I DO NOT UNDERSTAND
THE FEARING AND THE HATRED
THAT'S SPREAD ACROSS THE LAND
THE FEW OF THOSE WHO SEEM TO CARE
ARE LOOKED ON IN DISGUST
AS IF THERE'S SOMETHING VERY WRONG
AND SOMEONE NOT TO TRUST

71. WHEN AN ANGEL CALLS.

WHEN AN ANGEL CALLS YOUR NAME
THERE'S NOTHING YOU CAN DO
BUT GIVE YOURSELF UP GRACEFULLY
FOLLOW HER ON THROUGH
BUT WHEN SHE CALLS THE NAME OUT LOUD
OF SOMEONE THAT YOU LOVE
YOU WANT TO HOLD FOREVER
AND KEEP THEM FROM ABOVE.
NO MATTER WHEN THE CALL MAY COME
MORNING NOON OR NIGHT
YOU CANNOT RUN YOU CANNOT HIDE
YOU CANNOT EVEN FIGHT.
TAKE THE HAND THAT'S OFFERED
DO NOT BE AFRAID
YOUR FATE WAS SEALED WHEN YOU WERE BORN
THE PLANS ALREADY MADE
AND THOUGH YOU MAY NOT SEE IT
YOU MAY NOT UNDERSTAND
THERE'S NOTHING ELSE FOR YOU TO DO
BUT TAKE THE ANGELS HAND
TEARS WILL FALL LIKE RAINDROPS
AND GRIEF BE HARD TO BEAR
YOU'LL FIND THAT THERE'S A SHOULDER
OF SOMEONE WHO WILL CARE
SOMEONE WHO HAS BEEN AROUND
FROM THE VERY START
WHO KNOWS YOUR VERY HOPES AND DREAMS
DEEP WITHIN YOUR HEART.

72. SSSHHHHH!!!!!

FROM OUT OF THE PAST
COMES THE MEMORY AGAIN
HAUNTING ME, HAUNTING ME
CAUSING ME PAIN
SO WHY DID I DO
JUST WHAT I HAD DONE?
IT STICKS TO ME FAST
WON'T LEAVE ME ALONE.
IT FOLLOWS ME ROUND
WHEREVER I GO
MAKING ME WORRY
THAT MY PAST MIGHT SHOW.
JUST FOR A WHILE
I THINK IT HAS GONE
IT DOESN'T COME ROUND
BUT NOT FOR TOO LONG
SO WHAT IS THIS MEMORY
AND WHAT DID I DO?
MY SECRET STAYS WITH ME
I'M NOT TELLING YOU!

73. TRAVELLER

ONCE A YEAR FROM WHO KNEW WHERE
THE LADY WOULD APPEAR
WICKER BASKET ON HER ARM
A SMILE FULL OF GOOD CHEER
PEGS AND BRUSHES, DISH CLOTHS TOO
MOST WERE ALL HAND MADE
LUCKY HEATHER, GOOD LUCK CHARMS
THE THINGS SHE HAD TO TRADE
SHE NEVER STOOD AND CHATTERED
SHE WENT FROM DOOR TO DOOR
SHE SOLD HER GOODS AND THEN MOVED ON
JUST LIKE SHE HAD BEFORE
THE HORSES GRAZING BY THE ROAD
WERE FIRST SIGNS SHE'D BE ROUND
AND FURTHER ON THEIR CARAVANS
AND RUBBISH ON THE GROUND
A CAMP FIRE BURNING IN THEIR MIDST
CHILDREN RAN AND PLAYED
OLD MEN SAT AND SMOKED THEIR PIPES
AND NO ONE SEEMED AFRAID
THEY LIVED THEIR LIVES FROM DAY TO DAY
AND MOVED FROM PLACE TO PLACE
THERE ONE DAY THEN GONE THE NEXT
THEY LEFT WITHOUT A TRACE
YOU NEVER SEEMED TO SEE THEM
ONCE THEY'D MOVED AWAY
THEY VANISHED IN THE COUNTRYSIDE
WHO KNOWS WHERE THEY STAYED
THEN ONCE ANOTHER YEAR HAD PASSED
THE LADY WOULD APPEAR
HER WICKER BASKET FULL OF GOODS
A SMILE FULL OF GOOD CHEER

74. IF...

IF HANDS OF TIME STOPPED TURNING
COULD I GO TO MY PAST
WHAT WOULD I DO
WHAT WOULD I SAY
HOW LONG COULD I LAST?

IF I KNEW THEN WHAT I KNOW NOW
WOULD THINGS HAVE STAYED THE SAME
WHERE WOULD I BE
WHERE WOULD I GO
OR WOULD IT BE A GAME?

IF I COULD CHANGE MY HISTORY
KEEPING JUST THE BEST
WHAT WOULD I KEEP
WHAT WOULD I BE
AND WHAT ABOUT THE REST?

IF I COULD TAKE THAT STEP IN TIME
I THINK I'D LET THINGS BE
WHY MAKE CHANGES
WHY TEMPT FATE
I'D WANT TO STAY JUST ME.

75. T – T – F – N!

IT'S TIME ONCE MORE TO SAY FAREWELL,
TO SAY A SAD GOODBYE,
THE PAGES TURNED,
YOU'VE REACHED THE END,
DON'T BE SAD DON'T CRY.
I'LL COME BACK,
THERE WILL BE MORE,
BE PATIENT WAIT AND SEE,
GIVE ME JUST A LITTLE TIME
AND WHO KNOWS WHAT WILL BE.
SOMETHING DIFFERENT,
SOMETHING NEW,
I HOPE IT WON'T TAKE LONG,
BEFORE WE'RE ALL TOGETHER
STILL HAPPY AND STILL STRONG.
SO "T T F N!" I SHALL SAY,
ADIEU, BUT NOT GOODBYE,
TA, TA, FOR NOW,
I'LL MISS YOU ALL,
GOODNIGHT,
GODBLESS,
BYE-BYE.

www.ingramcontent.com/pod-product-compliance
Lightning Source LLC
Chambersburg PA
CBHW071738040426
42446CB00012B/2393